I was transported to the animal realm through *Walking With Mustangs and Other Wild Animal Tales*. I was given the opportunity to view another perspective. As humans, we filter our understanding of other kingdoms through our own life experience. Animals don't view or communicate through the limited pallet that we use. It was refreshing to read these heartfelt stories.

—*Karen Nowak, author of* Eye To Eye,
The Language of Energy and Horse

I like how *Walking with Mustangs*, opens with a closer look at Lloyd himself, his childhood, his love of animals (especially horses), his interactions with wild mustangs in Reno, Nevada, and some history about the introduction of mustangs into the West.

In the *Wild Animal Tales,* Chapters 2 through 13, Lloyd has a unique style that starts off as the narrator and then "shape shifts" to the point of view of the animal. Reading these tales, it reminded me of how Merlin would magically insert young Arthur into the bodies of various animals to afford him the knowledge of those experiences. I agree with Lloyd as he states in his epilogue that animals are more sentient than we may often give them credit for.

We dive into feeling what it's like to BE some of these animals in the wild—and a good variety of them, too. These tales are in the tradition of Jack London's *Call of the Wild*. While not for smaller children, they will make memorable reading for older ones—wonderful for reading aloud. The final tale ties it all back with a mustang who "joins up" with a friendly trapper. All in all, these are great adventures, with lessons learned, and enjoyable, eye-opening experiences to be had.

—*Denis Ouellette, author of* Heal Yourself
with Breath, Light, Sound & Water

My entire Alaska cruise group agreed that the short story, "The Bear," was absolutely captivating and wished Lloyd had brought more of his *Wild Animal Tales* to read to us.

—*Kathy Shoaf, Elite Cruises & Vacations Travel*

I picked up Lloyd's book one evening and got halfway through it. I found it hard to put down! It's an and interesting and fun read—educational too.

—Heather M. Gleen, Senior Proofreader
for Mule Deer Press

Lloyd Shanks' journey into print began decades ago in a one-room schoolhouse in California's Gold Country, when a teacher read stories about horses aloud to her class. His childhood ambition to one day own equines wasn't realized, but after he retired, a herd of Nevada mustangs brought his life to full circle. His experiences as an accidental horse-whisperer led him, Jack London-style, into the minds of other wild creatures. His book is part memoir, sprinkled with western history and natural history, with fantasy and fiction blended in. It's a record of the trek his heart has taken over many years. Shanks' work gives truth to the adage that "life has more imagination than dreams.

—Frank X. Mullen, Jr., author of
The Donner Party Chronicles

The *Wild Animal Tales* help us explore the psyches of animals that we humans often describe as powerless in their instincts. Lloyd points out that these animals may be more like us that we realize in their willingness to protect their young and fight for their lives. His writing also suggests that humans are only a single ingredient in our natural world. I enjoyed the reading!

—Hanna Massey, Montana State University graduate
in English Literature and Writing, pursuing
a Masters of Fine Arts in creative writing

Walking with Mustangs

and Other
Wild Animal Tales

Lloyd Shanks

BOZEMAN, MONTANA

Walking with Mustangs
and Other Wild Animal Tales

Lloyd Shanks

Print ISBN: 979-8-6689412-0-9

Published by
MULE DEER PRESS
3426 Lemhi Trail Drive
Bozeman, Montana 59718

Printed in the United States of America

Cover design and typeset by Denis Ouellette

❖ Dedication

This compilation of short stories is dedicated to the memory of Thornton W. Burgess, the first author whose name I ever memorized as a pre-teen, and to Whitefoot the Woodmouse, a gentle creature brought to life in Burgess's book by the same name. I read that book many times over, and his writings inspired me (over seventy years later) to write these stories about native wild animals of the north woods whose lives are intertwined, and also about two non-native animals who came into the Yukon Territory—one by choice and the other as a result of a mistake in direction, with an almost tragic conclusion.

While Mr. Burgess's gentle creatures speak, mine do not, and in my stories, their lives are linked by the laws of nature in a harsh environment, where both hunters and their prey live and die. So, while the books Mr. Burgess wrote—still available on the Internet today—are very much appropriate for young children, my short stories are intended for more mature readers who may have also appreciated the works of another great writer, Jack London, whose name I also memorized years ago.

—*Lloyd Shanks*

❖ **Acknowledgments**

When these stories were originally written, I didn't give much thought to ever publishing them. I owe a special thanks, therefore, to my self-publishing coach Denis Ouellette. Denis kept assuring me that *Walking With Mustangs*, originally written for family and friends, and *Wild Animal Tales*, written to share with the Writer's Group at the Bozeman Senior Center, were well worth combining and publishing.

Our hours of working together put into editing and communicating were what enabled the eventual completion of these short stories into a more professional publication. Denis also designed the cover and helped me to find, adjust, and place the great illustrations in this book.

I also owe well-deserved thanks to Linda Locke, who edited the work in progress and helped me spot several "senior moments" in the stories.

Much thanks also to my daughter, Karla, who assisted me with technical issues and helpful suggestions.

❖ Contents

Dedication iii

Acknowledgments iv

Preface vii

Introduction xi

1 • Walking with Mustangs 1

2 • The Bear 21

3 • The Wolverine 25

4 • The Bear and the Wolverine 29

5 • The Trapper 33

6 • The Pine Marten 43

7 • The Black Wolf 47

8 • The Snowshoe Hare 53

9 • The Caribou 57

10 • The Moose 61

11 • The Wolves and the Lioness 65

12 • The Lioness 71

13 • The Mustang 77

Epilogue 83

About the Author 87

❖ Preface

Walking with Mustangs sets the stage in my introduction with a historical account of how the horse species returned to North America and how "mustangs" repopulated in the Yukon.

Chapter 1 is the true story of my lifelong love of all horses and the "daydream" of someday owning one of those magnificent creatures. Although never realizing that dream, after retiring I was fortunate enough to live within walking distance of a band of feral horses in northern Nevada, visit them often, walk among them (getting toes stepped on from time to time) and finally form a bond with a few members of one herd. While I never considered myself a kind of "horse whisperer," there were ways to non-verbally communicate. I often scolded them loudly when they crowded too closely to grab the carrots or apples. In time, a mother and her twin colts welcomed grooming with a brush, even though none of the other horses did.

The *Wild Animal Tales* that follow in Chapters 2 through 13 are a collection of short stories from the animals' point of view that are the result of my appreciation of the writings of the late authors Thornton W. Burgess and Jack London. Although the characters in Mr. Burgess's books can talk to each other, mine only communicate non-verbally. I was informed that my first tale, "The Bear," was too visceral for some, but unfortunately that is the way of nature when both the predator and prey share the same environment. While stories like *Whitefoot the Woodmouse* were intended for a younger audience, my short stories about a number of different species of animals and a man living together in the Yukon back in the year 1946 are meant for more mature readers who appreciated the kind of tales Jack London wrote.

The place I envisioned for these stories is the sparsely inhabited northernmost border of the Canadian-owned Yukon Territory and the Territory of Alaska, acquired in a purchase from the Russians, who had once sent trappers to these northern coasts to trap sea otters. At that time, this purchase for $7.2 million was referred to as "Seward's folly." My stories are set in the year 1946, when the vast majority of land, on both sides of the border of the Yukon Territory, was home only to a great variety of wild animals, other than a few intrepid trappers from both the "First People"—Athabaskans—and a few hardy "whites."

No matter whether you were native or non-native, trapping fur-bearing animals was the only way to get the cash needed to buy whatever enabled you to comfortably live off the land here. Yes, there was usually enough wild game available to supply one with meat, but if you wanted any man-made things, like woolen socks, gloves, scarves, matches, candles, kerosene, canned fruit and vegetables, traps, ammunition for your rifle, a shotgun or pistol, or a new weapon of any kind, you trapped, skinned, and tanned the animal skins that were in most demand.

The snowmobile had not yet been invented, so a trapper had to traverse the miles of a trap line on a pair of snowshoes that he either made himself or was fortunate enough to buy. The rifle he carried was usually a weapon passed down from his grandfather, to his father, to him. Most of these were either old, well-used, lever-action or ex-military rifles.

In the spring and fall, the streams were full of migrating salmon that were being scooped out by bears and netted by humans. The former devoured them the moment they were caught, and the latter smoked and dried them for a valuable food supply in winter when wild game would be scarce. The caribou and black-tail deer all tended to migrate to the south of the Yukon, where the hardier fur-bearing animals were trapped, so they were not able to be hunted for food at that time. Although they were not found in large numbers, a lone moose provided so much meat, if one was lucky enough to have harvested one late in the fall, it would supply a single trapper for almost the whole winter.

So, life in the Territory was a struggle for both animals and men. It was an extremely hard place for both to live, and all the stories that follow are intended to illustrate that.

❖ Introduction

The Ancestral Horse

Some paleontologists maintain that the *Equinus* was originally a native of the North American continent and entered Asia by crossing the land bridge over the present Bering Straits. For some reason, after the land bridge disappeared under the rising sea, horses became extinct in their ancestral home and remained so for about one hundred centuries. Today thousands of these animals roam free through parts of the western United States. Herds of "wild" horses, called mustangs, are living free in parts of Arizona, Idaho, Nevada, New Mexico, Montana, Texas, and Wyoming. Where these horses came from, and how they came to roam together with other wild native species of North America, such as pronghorn antelope, mule deer, and desert bighorn sheep, is quite interesting.

The correct scientific term for these animals is "feral horses."

Ten thousand years after their extinction on this continent, horses were returned to the "New World" in the year 1494 aboard a sailing vessel on Christopher Columbus' second voyage of discovery. These animals had to be secured in place in slings aboard the vessel, and they had to be fed by-hand in order to survive the long voyage. When the ships finally reached the coast of "Hispaniola," the second largest island in the West Indies, the horses were pushed over the side of the ship and had to swim ashore.

The term *mustang* was derived from the word *mestisos,* meaning mixed breed. I found it fitting that a Spanish word was used to describe the kind of horses now roaming free in North America because, in 1540, horses were brought here with the mounted expedition led by the Spanish explorer Francisco Vazquez de Coronado. He entered what is now the southwestern United States in his search for the fabled "seven cities of Cibola." Those explorers were mounted on horses called "Spanish Barbs." Their horses were well suited for surviving in the hot and dry desert climate of what is now Arizona, New Mexico and western Texas, because they were direct descendants of the Spanish horses ridden by the "barbarians"—the Moors who invaded and conquered Spain in the eighth century.

Not every one of the Spaniards, who had traveled to the north from their new homes in Mexico, returned from their unsuccessful search for the seven cities of gold, and neither did their mounts. Those horses were the source of the first herds of horses domesticated by the Native Americans who, when they first saw them, thought they were giant dogs!

Numerous breeds of domesticated horses were imported to North America from England and Europe over the next two centuries and were destined to contribute to the bloodlines of the horses owned by the Native American tribes. Those people had no concept of land ownership, but they counted the number of horses you owned as a sign of great wealth—something a young brave could trade to his future father-in-law for the hand of his daughter.

Many of the horses were brought along the journey by the pioneers migrating to the west during the "western expansion." This was the politically correct term for the settlement of lands that were the sole territory of all of the different "wild Indian" tribes at the time. A number of those pioneers' horses either strayed or were stolen during the arduous journey westward. Some of these horses were "dray horses," descendants of breeds that had been huge "war horses," once ridden by knights in armor in England, Scotland and Western Europe. These horses were later used to pull plows, carts, wagons, and carriages. The pioneers migrating across North America valued both their dray horses as well as the smaller, saddle horses. However, any of those pioneers' horses were of an even greater value to the brave who could add them to his collection of smaller mounts. Naturally for him, any mare that could produce larger and stronger colts was the most desirable.

Here Comes the Cavalry

Other welcome additions to the bloodlines for those Native American herds were the hundreds of saddle horses ridden by the "long knives"—the United States Cavalry. The horses ridden by Native American "dog soldiers"—a term dating back to when horses were first thought to be large dogs—were called "Indian ponies" by the Cavalrymen because of their short stature.

Conversely, those bought by the Army to be ridden by the "troopers" tended to be much larger, taller and stronger animals that were intended to outrun and outlast the smaller mounts. That was not always the case, and it was a common practice for any trooper who came under heavy attack to knock down his horse and use it for cover during the ensuing battle. While many of their mounts were slain, foals from any surviving and captured mares were a most welcome addition to the "Indian pony" herds.

When those Native American tribes who owned horses were forced to move onto reservations, they were on foot. The United States government decided that they would have no need for their horses to hunt buffalo, because they were expected to eventually become farmers and raise their own food. Besides, horses would only make it easier for any "hostiles" to escape.

"Cow Ponies" *Remudas*

Finally, the last source of breeding stock to be assimilated into the bands of free-roaming mustangs were stray "cow ponies," most of which were originally captured and "broken" to become working horses for the annual roundups and cattle drives to distant rail yards. The cow ponies were brought on these drives in *remudas*—Spanish for the herd of saddle-broken horses from which ranch hands chose their mounts for the day. Some cow ponies strayed and returned to the open country, or they were spirited away in the night by resourceful mustang stallions bent on increasing their band of mares.

The American Feral Horse

Although many describe mustangs as wild horses, they are wild only in the sense that they roam free and have not yet become domesticated. Of course, when they are trapped and become cornered, they will rear up and lash out with their hooves when someone comes toward them. It must be remembered that horses are "prey animals," and this is how they defend themselves—so they are just being a horse! Numerous mustangs, rounded up annually by the Bureau of Land Management, or BLM as they are called in Nevada, are taken to the State Prison in Carson City for a program whereby they are "gentled" by inmates and readied for adoption by residents.

Because they are a mixture of breeds, the mustangs in a single, large herd may contain an amazing array of colors, described as albino, bay, black, buckskin, dun, paint (pinto), palomino, roan, or sorrel. The typical mustang's short stature is probably due entirely to the lifetimes of poor diet that its ancestors had to survive on. However, in the herd living near my home in Hidden

Valley, near Reno, NV, the "alpha mare" was a very large and muscular horse that was several hands higher and broader, in both the shoulders and hips, than the herd's stallion. She was probably retired from a modern ranch that showed off their wagon in parades and at rodeos and was set free to live out her remaining life on BLM land.

PS: The historical information regarding the reintroduction of the horse to North America was taken from *Cities of Gold* by Douglas Preston (Simon and Schuster 1992). This is an excellent narrative of the journey taken by two men on horseback who traced Coronado's route from the border of Mexico through the deserts and rugged mountains of Arizona and New Mexico.

1 ❖ Walking with Mustangs

Horse Daydreams and Wishes

There's an old saying that goes, "If wishes were horses, then even beggars would ride." In April of 1946, I was eleven years old. I was sitting in a one-room country schoolhouse in the crossroads town of Glencoe, California, in the middle of Calaveras County, located in the heart of the "Gold Country," where the two-lane highway from Mokelumne Hill to West Point forked. Railroad Flat, about twenty miles to the south, had a gas station and a church. The nearest grocery store was in Jackson, over thirty miles away. It could be said that West Point, California, was not the end of the earth, but you could see it from there, and Glencoe was far smaller. Actually, Glencoe was just a collection of ranches, and my white-clapboard schoolhouse was the only building that was not a ranch house.

Although it was not yet identified by science as a brain disorder, or understood by anyone, I had what is today called attention deficit hyperactivity disorder (ADHD). I daydreamed a lot in school, and it was often about owning a horse. After lunch each day, our teacher Mrs. Rader dramatically read a chapter from the book *Green Grass of Wyoming* by Mary O'Hara to our mixed-grade class of ten. It was a story of a young boy who domesticated a feral stallion.

On some days, two of the students rode horses to school. Mrs. Rader's son rode a pinto pony, and a tall frizzy-haired girl sometimes rode a large horse she called a "shire" to school and back. I really wanted a horse as well, but my dad said there was no way he could afford keeping one up. So I knew the most exciting ride I would ever have on the way to school would be hopping on the back of an occasional lumber truck from the mill at West Point. It first slowed enough to be shifted into low gear at the bottom of the steep grade a mile below the schoolhouse. Then my friends and I would jump off at the top of the hill as the driver would shift into second gear.

Still Horseless

Two years after my father and mother divorced, he remarried and bought a house in Stockton, located in the middle of California's central valley. Stockton sounded to me like it could be a cattle town with lots of cowboys and horses, but it turned out to be a marketing center for the surrounding farms that raised grapes, tomatoes, onions, and fruit trees. The only horses there were living at a riding stable where my stepmother used to ride when she was a girl. It was only a couple of blocks from our house, and the charge for an hour-long ride was two dollars.

My allowance for hand mowing, edging, and raking our very large lawn was only a dollar a week, so it took me two weeks to pay for a ride. I later started mowing two other lawns, and that money provided me with enough for a ride every week. I started hanging around the stables, hoping to get hired, but my time there came to an end when one of the horses tried to bite my finger off when he thought it was a carrot.

After becoming a teen, my interests shifted from horses to hunting, motor scooters, motorcycles, cars and, of course, girls. Then I graduated from high school, joined the Army, worked two years for Boeing, and attended and graduated from the University of Washington. We moved back to California, and I started working in San Francisco. My wife, our three daughters, and I lived in seven suburban subdivisions for the next thirty-seven years, and we never owned a piece of property suited for keeping a horse.

My wife and I decided I should take an early retirement and that we should move to Nevada. I was actually hoping to buy a small ranch in the Gold Country, but we changed our plans after visiting a couple who had sold their small winery and retired to a hilltop home nearby. They complained about the hour-long drives just to buy groceries or a needed piece of hardware. Also, the nearest hospital was miles away in San Andreas. Jan sensibly insisted that at our age we needed to be closer to a hospital, an airport, and (most important of all) a shopping mall. Since two of our daughters lived in Sacramento, we decided to look for a smaller home in Reno, just under two hours away.

Discovering Hidden Valley

In the 1950s film "The Misfits," Clark Gable and Montgomery Clift played a couple of low-life characters that chase a band of mustangs onto a dry lakebed. They lassoed one of them with a rope tied to a heavy truck tire, and when the horse became winded and could no longer run, they loaded it into a stake-bed truck to transport it to a nearby slaughterhouse. I hated that movie! That lakebed is located not far from Reno, Nevada, and the adjacent Truckee Meadows that lie east of the city.

In 1846, one of the members of a wagon train traveled a narrow wash down the Virginia Range. He wrote in his journal that they found "a great meadow of lush grass" upon which their cattle could graze until they had been refreshed after the ordeal of dragging their settlers' wagons across the forty-mile desert that had taken three days and two nights to cross. They would need the strength as they were heading over the steep pass across the Sierra Nevada mountains to the west.

Other wagon-train parties, who years later were on their way to California, described that same meadow as an "absolute quagmire." Whether it was a lush meadow or a swampy mess depended on whether or not the river had overflowed its banks the previous spring. Whenever it was a lush meadow, I am sure it was filled with more than one band of mustangs. Today that meadow is filled with the Reno Airport, the Hidden Valley Golf Course, McCarran Boulevard and a recently completed bypass parkway, both of which are four lanes wide.

In 1999, Jan and I were scouting for a home to buy in Reno. An ex co-worker of Jan's had retired and lived just east of Reno in an unincorporated community developed in the late 1960s, named "Hidden Valley" by its developers. As we drove toward Gary and Carol Brown's house, we crossed over a short bridge over a shallow stream of water

we later learned was named Steamboat Creek. Not far beyond the bridge, we spied a yellow warning sign that read: Caution Wild Horses on Road.

After we arrived at the Browns, I commented that I'd not seen any signs of horses and no sign of their droppings on the street. Gary said, "That sign is there for the occasional times when they get across the cattle guard. The horses used to come around all the time, and there were plenty of droppings on the streets and in many of the yards. On winter nights, the horses used to crowd alongside the houses to get out of the wind. The disgusted homeowners decided to close off Hidden Valley from the horses with a smooth wire fence. But I guarantee that you'll see plenty of horses soon enough."

We started to think that Hidden Valley would be a great place to relocate when I was able to retire. Almost every one of the hundreds of custom-built homes sat on lots graded out of a sloping "alluvial fan" of rocks and sandy soil at the base of the high hills that are part of the Virginia Mountain Range separating Reno and Virginia City to the southeast. West of those homes and the huge Hidden Valley Golf Course, Steamboat Creek flows from Rattlesnake Mountain towards the Truckee River, located a couple of miles to the north.

Like most of Truckee Meadows, Hidden Valley had been planted with thousands of trees. Even the treeless, camel's hump of Rattlesnake Mountain added to the rugged beauty of the surrounding area. Also, there were horses somewhere nearby! I couldn't wait to see them for myself.

First Sightings

As part of the visit, the Browns promised us a tour and drove us around the homes and then crossed a cattle guard and headed onto a rough, dirt-and-gravel road leading into open land. It had nothing but sandy soil, thousands of rocks, rabbit brush, and sagebrush covering the open land south of the development. We wondered where we were headed now. The Virginia Foothills loomed over a thousand feet above us on the left, and a wide ravine ran between two of them. After we had driven close to a mile, Gary took a left turn just before the ravine and headed his GMC Yukon SUV about a quarter of a mile up a rock-filled, four-wheel-drive road. When we reached the top of a bluff, we found the scattered remnants of an alfalfa hay pile surrounded by a herd of mustangs.

There were about twenty mares, a few colts, and a healthy-looking black stallion. When we got out of the vehicle, a mare with a very young colt moved away from us. The rest of the group stayed put, continuing their nosing at the remnants of hay on the ground. Carol told us that the hay was brought there by some ladies from Hidden Valley who solicited donations from the homeowners there and used it to buy alfalfa. I was told that those ladies had names for some of the horses, and their favorites were Rusty, the stallion, and Rebecca, the large alpha mare.

Because the ladies delivered the hay bales with a pickup truck, the horses always came to see what anyone who drove up in what sounded like a pickup had to offer. We were told that some families with children came with carrots and apples. I had a Toyota pickup and thought that I could bring my great-granddaughter there when she came to visit. Of course, planning ahead, I'd have to drive carefully around the biggest rocks since my pickup was only a two-wheel-drive.

Two hundred yards down the wash was another, smaller band of mustangs, consisting of a lanky roan stallion, two mares, and a runty-looking colt. One mare was hardly larger than her young colt and had a beautiful reddish-brown body, a blond mane, and a white blaze running from her forehead down to her nose. Her colt had a blackish-brown body and a reddish-brown mane. It was not an attractive color combination, but it is a good example of the mixing of genes within a mustang herd.

Then the roan stallion started walking up the ravine, toward the black's herd in what we interpreted as an apparent attempt to possibly add to his meager collection of mares waiting below. The black stallion moved downhill to position himself between the roan and the herd standing on the bluff above. All of the mares had turned their heads, as did we, to watch the unfolding drama that we thought was coming next. Perhaps we'd be a witness to the kind of vicious fight between stallions that we'd seen in films. What actually happened was far less dramatic. The black horse stretched out his neck as far as possible, pulled back his lips and bared an impressive mouthful of teeth. The roan, who obviously decided he was the weaker of the two, slowly turned and ambled back down the wash to his small herd waiting below.

After this tour, we decided we wanted to move to Hidden Valley someday soon and continue to be close to these herds and to hike in the hills above. I also vowed that next year, when I turned sixty-five, I would climb to the top of Mount Rose looming in the distant southwest. I daydreamed that if I would be able to adopt a small horse and board it nearby, I could use it as a pack-horse to hike some additional sections of the Pacific Crest Trail, which my son-in-law and I had hiked in my mid-fifties. I decided that the ideal mustang to adopt would be that beautiful mare with the odd-colored colt.

First Hike

We were now sure we wanted to move to Hidden Valley, but we just didn't know when. My employer, ANGUS Chemical Company, had been purchased by Dow

Chemical, and I was eligible for early retirement, but just when I could take it was up to Dow. About two months after our visit, the Browns had mailed us a sales brochure describing about two-dozen affordable houses being built on the south end of Hidden Valley within easy walking distance to where they drove us. Jan and I decided that retirement could not be that far off. We flew back to Reno and chose a house and lot.

Even though we bought the house in November, I was not able to retire and move until the following April. We spent that spring and summer laying sprinkler and drip lines, planting a small backyard lawn, planting numerous shrubs and eighteen trees on our lot. Early that November, I took two hikes into the hills above the wash without spotting a single mustang. I was told that the herds spend the summer up in the hills east of the Virginia Range, and they didn't come down into the valley until winter. Later that month, there was an early snowfall, and I decided it would be a good day for a hike in the snow.

After passing the wide wash, I turned east toward the range of hills. I spied two mustangs that were standing about two hundred yards to the south of where I had stopped to look at them, and they were both staring back at me. I wanted to get closer for a better look, but was afraid they'd run away. I started walking on again toward the base of the mountain, but as I moved ahead, they started walking towards me. After they came about one hundred yards closer to me, I changed my direction of travel, angling slightly towards the south, so we'd both be moving even closer together. When we were about forty yards apart, I stopped.

The two mustangs kept moving even closer, and eventually they were standing quite close to me. I'd read about a "join up," which means the horse comes toward you if you don't push it. Being a herd animal, horses will seek the company and protection of others (either other horses or man), provided they do not feel threatened. In the end, they moved within a few yards of me. It was quite a rewarding experience to have them trust me that way. Of course, maybe they were just very curious to see what I was up to.

One Herd Returns

The snowfall in the lower elevations around Reno tends to be fairly light and often melts the next day when the sun comes up. Most winter storms are "westerlies" that blow in from the Pacific and deposit most of their snow in the high Sierra Nevada Mountains beyond the valley to the west. The only heavy snowfall comes from a "northern slider" that blows all the way down from the Pacific Northwest. Up in the high country to the east, where the horse herds enjoy the much cooler summer weather, the colder winter temperatures drive the horses down to the valley where they spend the whole winter—undoubtedly wishing they could still huddle against those houses when the cold winds come down from the north.

On my next hike in the light snow, I found that a herd of twenty or so mustangs had returned to the bluff, and it was the herd that the stallion Rusty and the alpha-mare Rebecca ruled. The entire herd was busy feasting on a couple of bales of alfalfa hay that those kind ladies had undoubtedly dropped off a short time ago. As I turned back towards my house, I noted that their truck tires had left muddy ruts cut into the thin blanket of snow.

I returned to our house and then drove to a supermarket known for its bargains. They had some of the largest carrots I had ever seen in the produce bin, and they were a bargain. On the drive back, I noticed there were large bunches of tall, golden grass with long seed heads growing in a strip of land between the road and the chain-link fence surrounding that side of the golf course. I stopped and examined the large seeds. It was perennial rye grass, and at one time was undoubtedly a real treat for the horses before they were fenced off from Hidden Valley.

I had not seen any of this kind of grass out in the desert when I took my hikes, and I wondered if it could be grown anywhere in the vicinity near the places the mustangs wintered. This bunchgrass would need more water than the sparse grass, sagebrush, and rabbit brush was getting. Of course, the wash! Whenever it rained heavily, water ran down the middle of the wash, collected in any shallow places in the center and then sank into the sandy soil. Each winter, the snowfall on the shady south side of the wash melted slowly and kept the soil there fairly well moistened. I decided that this would probably be the best place to plant all the rye grass seeds I would be able to harvest.

Getting to Know You

After returning to the herd with my bag of large carrots, I slowly walked towards them. The first to notice the carrot I held in my outstretched hand was the large bay-colored alpha mare that the ladies had named Rebecca. She was, by far, the largest horse in the herd. She was taller, had broader hips, more muscular legs and bigger hooves than any mustang, and she would have made an excellent saddle horse, while many of the other horses there would not. This large horse may have been a descendant of another large horse used to pull a wagon or stagecoach in years gone by. A bay-colored colt trailed closely behind Rebecca. This colt was a yearling, probably born last winter or spring.

All of the horses in this herd appeared to be healthy—none had ribs showing, and they were muscular—but almost all of them were smaller than most domesticated horses. Their winter coats had grown thicker, but their manes and tails were tangled and had bits of brush and cheatgrass seed stuck in them. Other than that, one might think they were a large bunch of domesticated horses. They were, of course, unshod. However, none of their hooves were in need of trimming. The numerous rocks and sandy soil had kept their hooves worn down and, judging by the sound the hooves made when they struck the rocks, they were rock-hard.

It took no time at all for the other horses to smell the carrots, surround me, and quickly devour all that I had. I decided that buying carrots for them would be an infrequent event, but thought that after planting a couple of apple trees in my backyard I'd have plenty of apples for the herds in the future. I also thought again about the bunches of grass growing alongside the golf course.

First Annual Harvest

Horse owners in Kentucky rave about the "bluegrass," and I am sure that it provides their horses with tender succulent grazing each year. However, if I owned a pasture for horses, I'd seed it with perennial ryegrass. Here, this bunchgrass was growing in a mixture of poor gray soil and fine gravel along a roadside with no moisture other than an occasional spring rain and sparse snowfall in the winter. A single ryegrass seed can produce an amazing clump of grass at least eight inches in diameter with ten to twenty heavy stalks rising above its base. Each stalk produces an annual bounty of twenty or so seeds in the late summer.

It was early winter, and most of those seeds had not yet dropped. Perennial ryegrass sends down a thick base of roots and the clump of grass above can be grazed or burnt down each year, and the grass shoots come back strong and thicker again in spring. The bunch stays green through much of the summer, after the non-native "cheatgrass" has turned brown and put out their nasty sticker-like seeds that we used to call foxtails when we were kids. Those seeds had sharp points that always poked through your socks or got stuck in your dog's coat, tail and ears!

Bunchgrass used to cover much of the tall grass prairies of the American Midwest, and it survived trampling by herds of buffalo, prairie fires, and howling windstorms. It is a native grass and ideal for the dry lands in the west. Unfortunately, much of this grass has been displaced by non-native cheatgrass that came from China where it was used as a packing material in crates of breakable chinaware. There's an old proverb that states: "If the mountain will not come to Muhammad, then Muhammad must go to the mountain." Since all of the native bunchgrass was growing where the mustangs could no longer reach it, then why not gather the seeds and scatter them in a place they could grow?

The deep wash seemed the most likely place where the rich soil and annual runoff of water would make the seeds sprout next spring and hopefully sustain the grass through the summer. Before going to the trouble of harvesting the seeds, I decided to take a look at the wash to determine if my assumption about its growing conditions were right. It actually looked quite favorable for planting the seeds. The sandy soil was darker with minerals from the rocks in the wash above, and there were signs that water had collected in shallow pools in places. There were many rocks that had been washed down from the hills above, so I decided to stack a lot of them at the lower edge of those pool spots. These created small dams that hopefully would result in trapping more water. There was no doubt that the water would disappear into the sand; however, I had hopes that osmosis would transfer some of the water to the edges of the pool where I intended to scatter the seeds.

It took almost all of the next day to clip the seed heads and fill a large leaf bag with rye grass seed. Later that afternoon, I returned to the wash and started scattering seeds on the edges of the areas where I had created dams and kicked sandy soil over most of the seeds. I guessed the field mice might be satisfied with the uncovered ones and not dig up the rest.

Because the next few years were ones with very little rainfall in the west, and in spite of annual seed gathering, there was very little sign of new bunches of grass in the wash. Possibly the local field mice were the only ones satisfied with my efforts. Finally, we had a lot of rainfall the next fall and late snow in the spring. This caused the seeds I put out that year to sprout along the south side of the wash. So, I had hopes that this grass would put out their own seeds the next fall.

Making Three New Friends

The first time I drove out with carrots to the bluff above the wash, there was a young sorrel filly that came up to get her share. After all the carrots had been devoured, all of the horses except the filly left to resume their nosing around for some cheatgrass that was still green and edible. Then the filly started backing her rump up to the side of the pickup and rubbing it back and forth. I remembered I had a pair of rough leather gloves in the cab, so I retrieved them and went to her side. I was wondering if she would be spooked and kick back at me if I gave her a rubdown with the gloves. I stood to one side and rubbed her haunches with the rough gloves. Not only did she refrain from kicking me, she turned her rump to me. I thought, "What the heck, if that's what she wants, then let's give it to her!" I carefully rubbed her down on each side of her tail, being very careful not to soil my gloves. This lasted for about ten minutes, and then I gave her a gentle slap on her haunch, which told her, "That's all for today, sweetheart." I watched her slowly amble off. That just might have been the only massage that filly ever received, unless she ended up being adopted by a loving family. I'd like to think that's exactly what happened because she really was a sweetheart. That's when I decided to put an old, stiff-bristled hairbrush in my pickup.

The next time I returned, my niece and her young daughter came with me with some more carrots. I had the old hairbrush I'd removed from my pickup in the pocket of my field jacket. Ronette had her camera with her and started snapping some pictures, while her daughter sat in the back of the pickup and passed out all of the carrots. The herd was Rusty's, and Rebecca and her almost full-grown colt were among them. All three came up to the pickup and stuck their heads over the side of the bed to get their treat.

Another, very short and dark-colored (gray, brown, silver and black) mare with twin colts came toward us very cautiously. I took a handful of carrots and walked slowly toward them, holding out a tempting treat for the mare. She accepted it, but the colts did not seem to know what carrots were. I ended up giving the mare all of them, and then took out the brush and showed it to her. She sniffed at my leather glove and the brush but did not react, so I started to gently brush her back. It was obvious that this was something she was enjoying, so I kept brushing her more vigorously for at least fifteen minutes. Then

I started brushing one of the colts, and before long I felt a nip on the back of my pants leg. I turned and saw that it was the other colt. It was looking up as if to say, "Hey, I want some of that brushing too!" I ended up brushing both colts. When Ronette sent me copies of the pictures she took, one of the pictures was snapped just a moment before the colt was about to nip my pants leg.

A week later, I hiked out to see the horses. This time I had no carrots, but I did bring the brush. I walked up to the herd, and they all wanted to see what kind of treats I had brought them. I held out the brush and all of them walked away except the two colts. Both of them wanted to be groomed with my brush, while the rest of the herd nosed around the bits of alfalfa that remained on the ground after their morning feeding. After I was done with the grooming, I picked up a couple of handfuls of alfalfa for my two new friends.

A Really Sad Time

The next summer the Wild Horse Update column in the *Hidden Valley Newsletter* carried the sad news that Rusty had contracted West Nile virus and had to be put down. He was found lying on the ground, unable to get up. A vet was called. The vet determined the disease was just too much for the small stallion. He was given an injection to end his suffering. We later learned that both his alpha mare, Rebecca, and her daughter had joined up with another herd that was headed up by a stallion named Horseshack by the alfalfa ladies.

That fall, I brought my first crop of apples out to the wash. There were actually two herds there, and the larger of the two was Horseshack's. Rebecca and her young filly were still with him. After dumping half the apples for them, I walked over to the other herd, and found my three new friends among them. There was no doubt that the colts had matured enough to recognize the treats, and they crowded in for their share of them.

The following winter, there were even more horses wintering in the area between Hidden Valley and Rattlesnake Mountain. This put even more pressure on the ladies to buy more alfalfa. The BLM monitors the number of feral horses on federal lands in Nevada, much of which has little ability to sustain a large population of livestock. When the number of animals is too high for the range to support, they will round up a herd with helicopters and hold them in corrals until the healthy ones can be adopted. Unfortunately, the number of mustangs that get adopted each year is far lower than the number captured.

Because of their small size, many are not considered the ideal horse for an adult rider. However, I later learned that the open land surrounding Hidden Valley is not under the jurisdiction of the BLM, so no control of overgrazing is maintained there. Therefore, continued feedings of hay, plus whatever resulted from my efforts to seed ryegrass may be all that helped sustain the local mustang population near Hidden Valley.

Looking Back

In 2015, my wife was diagnosed with cognitive dementia (Alzheimer's disease), and we decided it would be best if we moved in with one of our daughters, so I could have some help with her care. We decided to live with our youngest daughter and grandson in Bozeman, Montana after having visited them on two vacations. In 2017, the four of us took a road trip to Reno, and we visited some of our former neighbors. We were told that during our absence, almost all of the herds of mustangs had moved south of Rattlesnake Mountain to an area where many new homes had been built. Apparently, the new lawns there were too tempting to resist.

I consider myself fortunate to have walked out among the herds as often as I did. It was the best thing, short of actually owning one of these survivors of the the West's colorful past.

2 ❖ The Bear

The bear was ravenous. She knew she had to leave her three young cubs alone in the den while she searched for something she could eat. She'd been nursing the triplets for a week and a half now, and she needed to nourish herself if she was going to continue to feed all three.

Although births of twin grizzly-bear cubs were fairly common among this species, a litter of three was more rare and caring for them would be hard. It was important to keep feeding the cubs, but equally important was defending them from attacks by predators. Boars (male grizzlies) were prone to attack, kill and eat any newborn bear cubs.

The den was near the top of a steep hill that overlooked a wide valley. Even though it was mid-spring, the valley was still covered with a foot of snow, and the stream running through its center was choked with ice. Spring came late at this height up the mountain, and the odds of the sow catching any small game were slim. A meager meal consisting of grubs and possibly some wild iris bulbs would probably have to suffice.

She carefully picked her way down the hill. It was covered with tons of rocks deposited by a landslide that had roared down the steep slope last spring, after a warm Chinook wind blew down from the peaks above and quickly melted much of the heavy snowpack. The snowmelt was so great that the runoff flooded a third of the valley below. This turned the lush meadow into a muddy marsh choked with cattails. Before she reached the marsh, she needed to cross an icy stream that flowed down the steep hill and turned to the south at its base, then dropped over a shelf of rock and formed a pool that was still iced over.

Near the far edge of that pool, frozen just under the thin ice, were two large trout, winter-killed fish. Because they had been frozen in the ice all winter, they'd still be edible. She devoured both in just a few swallows.

The next thing the hungry sow searched for was a fallen tree that might be full of the larvae of pine-bark beetles. She spied one and headed for it, but as she neared it, a large male grizzly rose up from behind the log, roared and opened his mouth to display a set of long, yellowed teeth. The boar was huge, but he was old, as indicated by the silvered hair around his snout and eyes. He was also not willing to share his meal with the female. He charged

after her. She knew the boar was a threat to both her and the cubs. Male grizzlies would often follow a sow to her den with the intention of killing and eating her cubs.

Her first instinct was to return to her den to defend the cubs, but she realized that the boar might succeed in injuring her, as well as killing all three cubs if she did. She would try to lure the boar away from the den while maintaining a safe distance from him. She was much faster than the older, heavier male and quickly began bounding back up the hill she had just come down. She angled away from the den as she traveled uphill. When she passed almost abreast of the den, the male turned away from her and headed straight for it. He probably caught the scent of either the cubs or the afterbirth she had swept outside the den with her huge paws a few days ago.

The female turned and raced toward the den. She reached it before the boar. She turned and positioned herself between the boar and the den's opening. Because the hill was steep, she stood uphill from the boar and was in the best possible position to fight him. Even though the male was taller, the female had a height advantage, as long as she could manage to stay uphill of him.

The boar roared in anger, drew his lips back to bare his teeth. He then lunged toward the female's throat. As his head drew nearer and was within her reach, she quickly stepped aside and brought her right arm down. She clawed the boar along the left side of his head. Her sharp claws raked his skull from the top of his snout, which was torn halfway off, to his eye socket. Blood gushed from both the top of his nose and his eye socket.

The wounds would heal in time, but he would always be badly disfigured and blind in one eye. After this fight, the boar might never attempt to go after another female's cubs again.

3 ❖ The Wolverine

The naturally reclusive female wolverine (called an angeline) decided that the bone-dry interior of this large hollow log would make a good den for this winter. She was pregnant and would probably have two or three kits this spring, but the odds were only one would survive to maturity. The Latin, or scientific, name for wolverines is *Gulo gulo* (or glutton). They are not a numerous species, and as a result, humans seldom see them. However, they are sometimes attracted to the bait that trappers hang above the traps set for Pine Marten (*Martes americana*).

She was a ferocious animal, and her kind has been known to drive off a bear from its kill. At a distance her bear-like shape could be confused with a yearling bear cub. But, when seen up close, her short snout and long tail put a quick end to that confusion. Wolverines have long and shaggy, multi-colored hair. It is not a very attractive pelt, black with auburn or blond streaks, but it is sought after for trim on arctic parkas because any frost that forms there can be easily be knocked off the thick hairs.

The male she had mated with was long gone, and he had not been seen anywhere in her large territory of about three hundred square miles for many weeks. A male wolverine would typically have a territory of as much as five hundred square miles, so the odds were good she would not see him again soon, if ever. Just like bears, wolverine mates do not live together after mating.

She was hungry, but there was only a very small chance of finding the kind of small game that she usually hunted for in the summer. She raised her short snout to search for the odorous smell of the picked-over carcass of a moose or deer, even though chances were there would be very little remaining of the latter. She could break any leftover bones with her strong jaws and lick the marrow from them.

If there was a cabin anywhere within her territory, she'd tear her way into it to raid it for any kind of edibles stored in the kitchen cupboards. She would leave absolutely nothing left uneaten or undisturbed. Also, if she happened to find a powdery item, like a sack of flour, it would not be eaten, but the sack would be torn open, and its entire dusty contents would usually be scattered all over the cabin and tracked all over the floor, while the animal searched the entire cabin to discover something tastier, like pancake syrup. Then, if she used her powerful jaws to puncture the thin sheet-metal "log cabin" container, the sticky syrup would leak out and a good deal of it might be absorbed by the flour on the floor. If this froze solid, the sticky mess would be impossible to remove until it thawed out. Woe be to the cabin dweller finding such a mess!

The only kill the angeline found in the vicinity was that of a small, black-tailed deer, which had already been torn apart and almost entirely devoured by a pack of wolves. Three wolves—two females and a young black male—were eating the only portion of the carcass that was of any size. When the angeline advanced toward then with her teeth bared, the wolves quickly backed off, not wanting to risk getting one of their leg bones snapped in two by the her powerful jaws. She quickly devoured the remaining scraps of meat on the haunch and then attacked the leg bones. When the wolves that had reluctantly surrendered the remainder of their meal heard the loud snap and crunch of the leg bones, they knew they had made the right decision.

Her hunger was somewhat satisfied. The wolverine was not in a mood to try to fight the entire wolf pack off if they arrived to finish off the meager remains of the kill. So, she turned her back and ambled off to return to the snug, new home she had found in the hollow log. She knew it would keep her dry all winter, and she would soon start to add bits of hair she would gather from kill sites to make a warm bed for her kits. They would be born nearly naked and blind, but within a few days their eyes would open, and in the next month their thick hair would start to grow out. They look very much like newborn bears when born, only smaller.

4 ❖ The Bear and the Wolverine

More than a month had passed since the grizzly sow had driven off the hungry grizzly boar. The spring weather was warmer and all three cubs were large enough to venture out of the den and follow their mother on one of her daily trips to forage for food.

All four of the bears emerged from the den into the warm sunlight and began making their way down the hill. The sow had to move at a much slower pace than normal, because her curious cubs were intent on exploring the landscape, smelling all the wildflowers and chasing every butterfly in sight. As they frolicked along, their mother searched the ground carefully for signs of vole burrows, and she found two of them. She dug them up, bit each of them once, and then swallowed the tiny creatures whole.

She was very hungry, and nursing three ravenous cubs made her much thinner than she was when she had to fight off the boar. She hoped there would be no sign of him today.

She thought that the easiest thing she could find for the cubs' first meal of solid food would be some pine-beetle grubs, and she knew that the old hollow log where she was surprised by the old boar should be full of them. The huge pine tree had been killed by an infestation of pine beetles after they'd burrowed under its thick bark. Years ago, a forest fire had burnt out a hollow that extended about seven feet into the trunk.

A large root ball had been wrenched from the earth when the tree fell and left a huge hole with dried roots sticking into the air. The cubs crawled into the hole and started to amuse themselves by climbing up the sloping edge of the hole and rolling and tumbling down its side to the bottom.

When the sow began ripping off slabs of dead bark to expose the grubs, she heard an angry snarl coming from inside the hollow log. She rushed to the end of the log, peered around the side of the roots and saw an ugly snout and toothy jaw just emerging from the dark cavern inside the log. It was a wolverine—the only small animal not afraid of a bear several times its size. The three cubs were at the base of the hole, and the sow thought the wolverine would surely attack them. Without a second thought, she jumped into the hole and positioned herself between the cubs and the angry wolverine, whose head and shoulders were just at the opening of the hollow log. When the wolverine's head had just emerged, the bear took a swipe at its nose with her huge paw, but she missed the small target.

In spite of her normally aggressive nature, the wolverine decided that fighting an angry she-bear with cubs down in a hole would be a battle she didn't have to undertake. She dodged under the bear, quickly scrambled out of the hole, and shuffled off with a slow and awkward gait. Even though a wolverine is shaped somewhat like a bear, they are far less agile and cannot run nearly as fast. Of course, there was little need for speed, because the bear decided there was no reason to pursue such an aggressive creature and risk a nasty encounter.

The pregnant wolverine had not eaten anything since yesterday morning, and her appetite was getting the best of her. She was anxious to find an easy meal, if she could. Wolverines are gluttonous, and any bit of carrion, no matter how rank or spoiled it might be, would satisfy her. Some folks call them skunk bears because they can carry the horrible smell of a rotting animal carcass on their fur.

The only thing she found to eat in the vicinity was the remains of a moose calf that had already been mostly devoured by a pack of wolves. All but a few tiny shreds of meat, sinew and bone were left, and after the wolverine finished devouring the scraps, she was still quite hungry.

She had only gone a short distance before she smelled a bit of caribou fat hung on a pine tree branch that was low enough to reach if she stood on her hind legs and reached up with her front paws to pull it down. Just as she did this, there was a loud snap, after she stepped on the pan of a steel trap that had been set directly under the bait and carefully concealed with a covering of dry grass and small twigs. The wolverine cringed with pain as the horrible device bit into one of her hind legs.

All through the night, the wolverine struggled to get free of the trap that was securely anchored with a chain. The more she struggled, the more the trap bit into her leg. She was cold and her leg hurt. She drifted off into a restless sleep, not knowing what the morning would bring. Her last thought was—if only that bear hadn't disturbed her sleep and chased her away from her nest in that cozy hollow log!

5 ❖ The Trapper

As the trapper passed this familiar bend in the trail, he vividly recalled his last sighting of the young cinnamon-colored female grizzly. She had kept to her den late in the season and had probably been nursing one or two cubs. Some bears seemed to repeatedly have twins, and she just might be one of them. He knew that it was nature's way of repopulating a species that had neared extinction in a particular territory.

Even though she was one of the species that a man should take care to avoid any close contact with, she was never aggressive towards him the numerous times they'd met while he ran his trapline. Of course, he'd been careful to never try to approach her when she was out with her cubs. That was something he knew was likely to trigger an attack, at least by some sows with cubs. Whenever he could, he'd always left a large strip of salmon skin and fat hanging upon a high branch near the places he had seen her roaming around his trapline. This was his way of rewarding her good behavior.

A month ago, he'd seen her on that ridgeline above him. He had also spied a huge male grizzly not far away. This bear had dark-colored fur with a gray tinge and was busy digging for roots in the meadow below. It wasn't a bear he had seen before in this part of what he considered his territory. Of course, in this part of the Yukon Territory, no human usually owned any territory except the small piece of land his cabin sat on. Even that place was not safe from an invasion by a grizzly or a wolverine. Their sharp claws and strong jaws could tear open wood shutters and even strong doors.

More than once, he'd decided to pepper the inside of the thick planks of his own cabin door with a blast from his twelve-gauge pump shotgun, loaded with birdshot that he used to hunt ptarmigan, a northern grouse of the mountainous and Arctic regions. One shot discouraged most would-be invaders.

The trapper had been careful to give the male bear a wide berth as he skirted around the meadow by following a hogback ridge. This had given him a good view of the valley below. Out of the corner of one eye, he'd noticed that the female had started moving down the hill. In this territory trappers always had to be aware of everything around them because they were definitely not on the top of the food chain. The female grizzly had been alone. It was early in the year, and her cubs were probably still in the den. As the trapper went along the ridge, he'd kept track of both of the bears, scanning the ground ahead of him to avoid stepping on dead branches that could snap and alert either bear of his presence. The wind had been blowing past the bears and toward him, so neither bear had smelled him or the scent of the bait he carried. After he reached the thick stand of spruce growing at the far end of the ridge, he gave the two bears one last glance.

The male had stood up and was staring at the female moving towards him and the hollow log she was rapidly striding towards. The smaller sow had stopped, stood up on her hind legs, and stared long and hard at the boar. That's when the boar gave out a roar, dropped to all fours, and raced up the hill toward the female.

The trapper could tell the smaller female was faster than the heavier boar and would probably outrun him. She had already reached a point near the top of the hill before the boar, and she turned to face him as he neared her. Then, she and the boar topped the hill and passed out of sight around the other side of an outcropping of large boulders. He had always wondered what the outcome of that encounter had been.

The sun crept a bit higher this morning as the trapper continued on his way toward his trapline, travelling along on his well-worn trail. His traps were all set on tree branches that he'd baited with some strips of fatty caribou hide to attract pine martens, the North American species resembling a weasel. These small, predatory mammals had winter coats of glossy dark-brown fur tinged with cinnamon-color highlights and an orange patch under their chins. The pelts were always sought after for trim for the neck and cuffs of ladies' winter coats and brought a high price on the fur market. Pine martens were quite active in the winter, and their fur was always in the best of condition during that season. It was well into spring at these latitudes, so this morning was the last time that he would check and remove all of the wire-noose snares he'd set on the upper tree branches to trap any curious marten.

Last week, he'd set his first steel traps below some baits hung in the trees to attract timber wolves. Wolves were smart, always cautious, and were hard to trap. However, their fine winter pelts brought high prices on the fur market. In a few weeks, all the ice should be melted off the beaver ponds, and hopefully he'd be trapping a lot of them this year. At the end of next month, the trapping season would end, and he would start fishing for salmon, trout and grayling, and drying his catch. Living off the land by himself was hard work, but it was the only life that he thoroughly enjoyed.

The first two traps he checked were empty, but the next two each had a marten in them. Both were dead because they'd been caught by the neck. There were times when an animal that was caught by a leg had chewed it off in order to escape. Seeing this, he hated having to make his living as a trapper, but there was no other way to earn money in this part of the Yukon, and he could not bring himself to give up this solitary lifestyle and relocate to some town where there might be work. Moreover, he was certain that there was no way he could ever survive a life in any Canadian town or city. A solitary lifestyle was all that he was really cut out for, and there was probably no white girl who could tolerate this sort of life in the woods. Of course, if he was lucky, he might find a native Alaskan girl who could. However, all the ones he had met whenever he visited the nearest town to buy supplies, wanted to move to an even larger town or a big city and get a job.

When he approached the first trap he'd set for wolves, he saw that he had caught a much larger animal by the rear leg. The animal was large enough to have risen up on its hind legs to reach for the bait. The trap had closed on one of its paws and held the dark-furred animal securely by one leg. Of course, it was frantic to get loose and was clearly angered by the predicament it found itself in. The animal was snarling and tugging at its trapped leg as hard as it could. From this distance it looked like it might be a young bear cub, but it was larger than one of this year's cubs and smaller than a yearling would be. As he got a little closer, he caught the animal's scent. Its smell was as strong as a skunk, but clearly it was not one. Then he recognized the odor—just like rotten meat—it was a wolverine!

Nothing could compare to the ferocity of a trapped wolverine, not even a riled bear. The trapper was not interested in adding this animal's odorous pelt to his catch, but he was clearly going to have to kill it. He would risk an injury to himself if he didn't shoot it with his rifle, but he was reluctant to waste even one precious round of his rifle ammunition on this beast. He had only two rounds left from the last box of fifty .22-caliber rifle cartridges he had purchased at the end of the trapping season last year, and he would need those if he was going to trap a wolf. He could probably club the wolverine to death with a stout stick, while it was held fast in the trap, and he turned to break a dead branch off the closest spruce. Just then, the wolverine tore its foot loose from the trap and turned. It rushed toward the trapper with an angry snarl.

The trapper heard the angry beast advancing toward him from the rear. He quickly snapped the nearest dead branch off the tree. He wheeled around, aware that if the vicious animal ever closed its powerful jaws around one of his legs, it could tear the muscle loose with one twist of its neck. As the wolverine quickly rushed at him, the man brought the club down on the animal's head as hard as he could. The dead branch snapped in two and became useless as a defensive weapon. However, the animal was stunned momentarily. This gave the man enough time to withdraw his large Bowie knife from the sheaf on his belt. Before he could stab the angry creature with his knife, the animal lunged forward and closed his powerful jaws around the trapper's ankle, right above the top of the low-top hiking boot he was wearing.

He felt the sharp teeth punch through his skin and heard the awful crunch of his anklebone being broken as the wolverine's jaws closed down on them. Before the animal could make any attempt to tear the ankle apart and wrench the foot off, the trapper plunged his knife down into the beast's back and severed its spine.

When he pried the dead animal's jaws from his ankle, the trapper saw a steady stream of blood flowing from one of the puncture wounds. A vein had been opened. If it had been a punctured artery, the wound would have been spurting blood with each heartbeat.

He removed his belt and used it as a tourniquet above the knee to stop the blood flow. He cut off one of the sleeves of his wool shirt to use as a bandage, tying it as tightly as he could around his ankle. When he stood up, sharp pains stabbed up his leg if he put any weight on it. He was sure he had sustained some bone damage. He hopped over to the tree on his good leg and broke off another long branch from the spruce that he could use as a cane. He then hung his backpack and rifle in that tree, knowing he could return later to locate and retrieve them after he had received the medical attention he sorely needed.

The injured man would have to hobble the two miles back to his cabin. Each time he tried putting any weight at all on his injured ankle, the pain made him lift it, and he hopped the entire way to the cabin. However, by the time he had arrived, both the wool shirtsleeve he had wrapped around his ankle and his heavy woolen sock were completely soaked with blood.

He felt lightheaded from shock and loss of blood. He knew he had to staunch the flow before he lost much more and passed out. He had everything he needed in his medical kit to do this and started to work. First, he cut a small amount of gauze and rolled it tightly, shaping it on one end, which enabled him to push it into the puncture hole with a cotton swab on a long wooden stick. He had used many of these to clean the action of his rifle that was now hanging high in a spruce tree.

Then he made a thick pad of cotton, placed it on top of the gauze plug, and used an entire roll of gauze to wrap the injured ankle and then, on top of that, he tightly wrapped an elastic bandage. This not only stopped the flow of blood, but it provided his ankle with enough support to allow him to put a little weight on it.

He threw the blood-soaked shirtsleeve and wool sock into the wood stove and put on a new sock, along with the high-top shoepacks that he normally used in deep snow. He laced it as tight as he could to provide extra support for his injured ankle, which by now was as numb as a piece of wood. This was good, he thought, because it would enable him to hobble the five miles to the Canadian Mounted Police winter cabin and ask them to call in a bush pilot to fly him to the hospital in Whitehorse.

When the trapper finally arrived at the mountie's cabin, the officer was fortunately there, rather than out in the backwoods looking for any poachers who might be hunting moose out of season. After the mountie examined and praised the excellent job the trapper had done to entirely stop the flow of blood, he got on the radio and called the closest bush pilot. The man had just returned from one of his supply flights and had just refueled his Cessna and was able to get in the air within minutes after getting the call.

Just over an hour later, the trapper was lying in the emergency room at Whitehorse, and the on-duty doctor was telling him what an excellent way he, as an amateur, had treated a very serious wound. He gave the trapper a tetanus shot, a bottle of antibiotic pills, and some strong painkillers. After he fashioned a walking cast, the doctor insisted that the trapper go back to the trapline site, cut off the wolverine's head and have the pilot fly it back to Whitehorse for a rabies test.

The trapper was then flown to a landing site near the trapline. He hiked back to where he had left the dead animal while the pilot waited for his return. He was relieved to find his rifle was still hanging in the tree and that no scavengers had disturbed the wolverine's carcass. The trapper not only removed the head they needed for the rabies test, but he also quickly skinned the animal, rolled up the odorous pelt inside a burlap sack, and stuffed it in his backpack.

A few days later, a passing pilot dropped a note in an old white sock weighted down with a rock at his cabin site. It carried the welcome news that the result from the rabies test was negative. The relieved trapper was then finally able to scrub and soak the smelly hide in a bucket of water with half a bar of lye soap for several days. He then rinsed it and tacked it on a board to sun-dry in the frigid air long enough for the rotten meat odor to disappear. He decided not to sell that pelt, even though it was quite valuable, since wolverines were reclusive, rarely seen, and seldom trapped. He decided instead to tack the pelt to his cabin wall as a trophy of the animal that could have killed him—if he had not killed it first. It would also

be a constant reminder of the solitary and stimulating life he'd chosen here in the wilds of the Yukon Territory.

6 ❖ The Pine Marten

The American pine marten is the smallest but possibly the most agile predator in the Yukon forest. As the name indicates, they live in a pine trees. This voracious species' territory includes mountain ranges from Montana all the way north to Alaska. Pine martens are a member of the animal family that includes badgers, skunks, weasels and, largest of all, wolverines, but they are the only one in that family with retractable claws like a cat. This enables them to rapidly climb pine trees and to scramble along the branches to catch squirrels, their primary food source, and quickly dispatch them.

The female pine marten is active in the winter and does not hibernate like her prey. A beautiful, thick, auburn coat, which is soft as down underneath and has a top layer of thicker guard hairs, keeps her quite warm through the bitter winter weather. Her dark fur, plus a blaze of golden-orange fur on her throat, is an indication that she is not a weasel, which are a lighter tawny color.

The pine marten is agile and leaps from tree to tree searching for squirrel nests. Typically, any occupants scramble out in an attempt to outrun her, but she usually catches them by the back of the neck, and her sharp, needle-like fangs put a quick end to most chases. However, if the prey stays put and bares its teeth to defend itself, she will have a much harder time getting it out of their hole to end the battle. Even small rodents like squirrels can mount a fierce attack to defend themselves when it is their time to fight or die!

Pine martens are very curious. Trappers will hang a strip of hide with fat or flesh attached to a pine-tree branch to attract and trap them. Their soft pelts are not large, but valued as colorful trim for ladies' coats and jackets. Many trappers' sets have a wire-loop snare around the bait, and when the marten sticks its head in and tries to jerk the bait loose from the branch above it, it is caught quite securely by the neck. The harder the animal struggles, the tighter the noose closes, causing the animal to suffer an unfortunate death.

That is what occurred this sunny winter morning after the marten was thoroughly unsuccessful in finding and routing out any squirrels. She spied a strip of caribou hide containing both flesh and fat and could not resist trying to pull it loose from the branch it was hung on. She failed to notice the thin wire noose and was soon hung by the neck, only to quickly expire.

Her body would be discovered the next day, not by the trapper, but by another, much larger and ravenous predator.

45

7 ❖ The Black Wolf

This healthy, young, male black wolf had been driven from his pack by the new alpha male that had fought and killed his father in a vicious fight for dominance last week. It was nature's way of ensuring that the strongest and healthiest animal was the dominant member of the pack.

His father had been the alpha male of the pack for many years, but had grown old and weak. It was time the pack had a much younger leader that had been born and raised as part of another pack. This eliminated the problems that resulted from inbreeding and led to many of the sightings and tales of the "lone wolf." These were almost always males, but sometimes a pack's alpha female would have driven off another female, or an occasional unruly young male pup that had been unwilling to submit to her dominance as she enforced the unwritten rules of wolf behavior.

Although many timber wolves are gray or white, this male was coal black with bright yellow eyes. He thought the striking color of his fur would surely be able to attract the attention of some young female to mate with, and he would either be permitted to join her pack or attract her away and start his own pack. Only time would tell which one of those that would be. Of course, at his young age he had never mated before, and the rites of wolf courtship were beyond him. Perhaps an older female might take the initiative and lead him on, if he was lucky.

He traveled east for two days after leaving his former pack's territory. If they had not made a recent kill, on any given day, wolves in a pack would range for many miles in any direction from their starting point to search for large prey to chase down and kill, such as a caribou or a moose calf. Of course, a pack would not hesitate to finish eating the kill of another animal, even to the point of crunching up any remaining bones with their strong jaws and teeth to get to the marrow. The black wolf, however, had not found any sources of nourishment for two days, and was now on the hunt for any small game he could find outside their winter burrows. At this time of year in late winter, most species of small game were currently curled up deep in their burrows for hibernation, but he just might be fortunate enough to find the large tracks of a healthy snowshoe hare out for a meal of tender, new-growth ends on some blueberry bushes or young willow trees. Of course, if a wolf became hungry enough, even the soft ends of spruce branches could be eaten to fight off hunger pangs. However, that would be his last choice before starving to death.

Sadly, there were no tracks anywhere to be found in this part of the territory. There were some beaver dams in some iced-over ponds, but only a hungry grizzly or wolverine would be strong enough to rip their wood and mud lodges apart in order to reach the beavers deep inside.

Suddenly, he caught the scent of a long strip of caribou skin and fat hung on a branch above a steel trap. The trapper had set and covered it with strands of moss and a dusting of snow, just below the bait. The black wolf's mother had shown him how to approach such a setting. He stretched out his neck as far as he could to avoid triggering the dreaded steel jaws of the trap. The young wolf approached the set warily, his mouth watering from the smell of the bait. He was just able to stretch his neck over the trap and snag the end of the skin to yank it loose.

The dead branch the skin was hung on snapped and fell on top of the trap. It was heavy enough to trigger the small, steel pan in the center of the two jaws with a loud snap. The wolf was alarmed by the noise and jumped back, releasing his hold on the strip of skin. It was some time before he got the will to slowly approach the sprung trap. He slowly stretched out his neck and was barely able to get his lips around the end of the skin. As he pulled down on the skin, a large icicle broke off the branch the wire was wrapped around and flew downward towards the wolf's head. To avoid it, he pulled back quickly and dropped the skin. Surely this quest for such a meager morsel was far too risky, and he gave up his efforts to retrieve the strip of skin.

He skirted the beaver pond, crossed over it on the dam of willow sticks and trunks, and circled the other side. There he was able to find several winter-killed perch and eagerly gobbled them up. They had not been locked in ice for the last three days and were a rather odorous meal, but the wolf downed every bit of the fish, fins and all. His strong gastric juices would dissolve every part of what he had just swallowed, just as it would have done for bits of bone or animal hide, and convert it to energy. But the three small perch did very little to curb the wolf's voracious hunger. He had to find something else to eat. Another scent of a dead animal was on the air. This time it was the small carcass of a dead pine marten hanging from a stout branch of a tree by a wire snare.

The trapper had set a hanging wire noose just beneath a piece of caribou hide and flesh. The wolf was not familiar with a wire snare, but because it was held tightly on the marten's neck, it seemed not to be a threat. The wolf grabbed the carcass and pulled on it with all of his might. This resulted in the beheading of the dead marten, but that was of no concern to the wolf, since the head was not something he would usually eat. Only the brain contained any food value. But this was not a normal time, so after he had consumed the rest of the body, the wolf went back to tear the head off the wire. As he bit down on the meager morsel still hung on the wire, the wolf tasted the acrid taste of the steel wire. He spat out the head and decided that it was something he didn't need to eat, in spite of his initial desire to do so. He also caught the scent of the trapper's bare hand on the wire. That scent was one he would remember. It would be stored in his brain as something to always avoid, or he too might end up in a snare like the dead pine marten.

After leaving the snare, the wolf continued on his quest to find others of his kind. Before long, it started to grow dark, so he decided to bed down for the evening. He found a snow bank that had piled up along one side of a spruce tree with branches that drooped to the ground, which would provide a welcome shelter to rest that night. But then he heard the howls of a wolf pack chasing some kind of prey about half a mile downhill from his location. If he started on his way now, he might catch up with them and share in whatever it was that they were chasing and hopefully taking down.

He was in luck when he got to the bottom of a ravine and saw the pack and what they were busy tearing apart. After once having seen this happen, the young wolf knew that he would be attacked if he dared approach the freshly killed black-tailed-deer fawn that was barely large enough to feed the pack surrounding it.

Even though the young wolf laid down quite a distance from the feeding pack and was waiting for them to finish tearing apart the remains of the deer, the alpha male stopped feeding and slowly walked towards him. The alpha's lips were parted, and his teeth were bared. The hackles on his back were standing up, which made him appear even larger than he was. The young wolf knew he was no match for the much larger male, so he sunk down as low as possible and rolled over to expose his vulnerable underbelly to indicate he was submitting to the authority of the alpha male. After standing over the younger wolf for over a minute, the alpha turned and slowly walked back toward the feeding pack. When he was halfway back to what was left of the deer carcass, he turned and looked back towards the young male. His mouth was closed, and the hackles on his back were no longer raised. This was a sign of the newcomer's welcome as the newest member of the pack.

As the black wolf moved toward the few remaining parts of the kill, the youngest female wolf in the pack moved to one side to allow the young male to take a bite of the haunch her mother had just fought over and secured for the two of them to eat. The young male whined to signify his appreciation of the welcoming gesture made by a newfound friend. Instinctively, the young male knew he had found both a new pack and a potential mate. As he looked for a good place to bed down for the night, he thought maybe tomorrow he would be allowed to join the pack in a hunt.

8 ❖ The Snowshoe Hare

He was fairly old as wild rabbits go. He had lived so long due to his acute awareness of any danger when it happened to arrive in the form of an ace predator, such as a weasel or a wolf. His excellent hearing, of course, was the result of what nature provided in the form of huge ears. Also, the speed with which a snowshoe hare could escape, thanks to strong, muscular hind legs, was another important factor that had led to his survival here in the Yukon Territory. Yet another factor was that his snow-white coloring disguised him well in the winter snow. Finally, he was often able to scramble into a thicket of heavy brush that the large predator could not enter. Of course, when he was pursued by a weasel, that was not an effective way to escape and neither was a retreat to his den in the ground. He was fortunate there were no weasels living near his habitation.

There were other kinds of predators he would have a hard time escaping if they ever sunk their talons into him. Those were the winged predators, like the great horned owl or the red-tailed hawk, and any number of other raptors. So, considering the many threats to his longevity, he really had been an extremely lucky rabbit!

Today, he was concerned because he knew there had been a wolf in the area last night. He smelled the acrid scent of urine where the animal had marked his territory on an aspen tree trunk and caught a whiff of the animal's musk where it might have bedded down for the night below a large spruce tree. So, the hare was on high alert as it quickly left that vicinity and headed for a safer area to browse on the bark of some young willows. At least he thought it was a safer area. As it turned out, it was just the opposite—a direction he should avoid.

Last night a heavy snowfall had covered the wolf tracks on the game trail the hare followed toward the willow thicket. If they had been visible, as they were earlier last evening, that was the last place the hare would be heading.

As the hare neared the thicket, his sixth sense alerted him that there was something watching him. He would have known it was the wolf had the predator's tracks still been visible. Of course, that was one of the hazards of living in the Yukon Territory in the winter. Even though the wolf had crouched low under a spruce, the one thing he could not hide in the white landscape was his jet-black fur. The hare spotted this in an instant and was immediately running at full speed toward some thorny wild-blackberry bushes. He dove under the lowest branches just before the pursuing wolf had to give up the chase or risk certain impalement on the sharp thorns.

The hare was ready to stay put for as long as the wolf was waiting outside his refuge. The wolf waited patiently for two hours, then turned away and went on a hunt for an easier catch.

9 ❖ The Caribou

The caribou herd moved slowly across the wind-swept tundra. They were feeding on the tops of dried grass that had grown tall enough last summer to be reached when these North American reindeer scraped through the covering of snow with their great racks of broad-tipped antlers. (The caribou is the only member of the deer family where both males and females grow antlers.) The large herd was on the move every day in order to find the supply of grass or moss they needed to stay alive.

Life in the northern edge of the Yukon Territory is extremely hard for any prey animal. Caribou rely on the sheer numbers in their herd for their primary means of protection when hunted by the packs of wolves that always seem to be waiting to stampede the herd and pick off the weakest animals that fell behind the fleeing horde.

Those were either the oldest or youngest animals, or those that were the least healthy. Of course, this was nature's way of keeping the strongest and healthiest breeding stock alive, and lessening the ever-present threat of over-population on their range, with the inevitable, widespread starvation that would follow.

And wolf packs were not the only predators. A tribe of Athabascans, natives who lived nearby and had hunted in this area for centuries, relied on the caribou for a steady diet of protein. They hunted with modern weapons, or at least some of them did. The two best shots in the tribe relied on weapons that dated back to a time when their great-grandfathers were the hunters. The oldest weapon was a bolt-action (7.62-millimeter or a .30-caliber) Russian sniper rifle that was built in 1905 and used in the short war between Russia and Japan. It had a very short, telescopic sight, and the current owner was a young native woman who almost always scored a lethal hit with it. It had been passed down in her family for years. It was ancient but was also a well-maintained weapon.

However, the most accurate and treasured rifle owned by a member of the tribe was one recently acquired by a young Athabascan man on a visit to a young lady from his tribe who had moved to Seattle. He had gone into a pawnshop and found they had a 6.5-by-55-millimeter-caliber Swedish Mauser in like-new condition that had been pawned by its previous owner for only $125 dollars. The famed Husqvarna Group had manufactured it in 1942 in Sweden. An adjustable "peep sight" had recently been mounted, and there was also a circular brass tag screwed onto the side of its butt stock that indicated its barrel was bored to only 6.49 millimeters. Both of these contributed to this being an extremely accurate weapon, and its new owner had won quite a bit of money in a shooting contest with some other members of the tribe, including the young woman who had thought that her old Russian sniper rifle was more accurate.

This morning it was bitterly cold, and there was a forceful north wind blowing sub-zero air down from the Arctic Circle. The hungry wolves were not up to leaving their beds in the snow to hunt, and none of the Athabascans wanted to venture outdoors today. As a result of this inclement weather, neither of the owners of those two rifles would be demonstrating their skills on a caribou hunt today.

10 ❖ The Moose

He was a strong, young bull of about four years old. After he'd finished pulling up and consuming all of the pond lily bulbs that were growing in the recently-thawed, shallow pond nearby, the moose bedded down for the night in a stand of willow bushes growing alongside it. With the water on one side and a thick growth of willow trunks all around him, he felt safe from an attack by the band of wolves he heard howling from the other side of the ridge. There was only one way into this thicket, and that was the way he had entered last night when he trampled his way in. Only one wolf at a time would be able to get to him, and they would be quickly disabled by one or two kicks of his broad hooves. These hooves were the reason the huge animal could walk through the thick mud and ooze on the bottom of the many ponds nearby without sinking and being trapped there. The howls of the pack were growing fainter now, so the moose knew they were moving to the east or south and away from him. This meant he would be able to sleep until the welcoming sunrise without fear of attack.

He was able to doze until the first rays of sunlight penetrated the bare willow branches, and he woke up hungry and ready to move on to another pond. The sun's rays were at a low angle this time of year, and provided light but little warmth, but his extremely thick hide and dense hair provided all the warmth he needed this morning. In the sub-zero days of winter, he might be shivering to help warm his body, just like the caribou did when they were not running away from a pack of wolves at full speed.

The moose was not able to run that fast, but he had his wide rack of horns and heavy hooves to defend himself. These had broken the ribs of more than one attacking wolf and driven off an entire pack on another occasion. Because his mate had lacked a set of horns, she had not been able to conduct an effective enough defense against a large pack of wolves and had been devoured a month ago—possibly by the same pack he heard last night. Naturally, there was no way to tell one pack from another, unless it had a member that was not grey but snow-white or black.

On his way to the next pond, the moose stealthily moved past an Athabascan village. They had already started their morning cooking fires, and the women were busy preparing a meal for their men and children who were still in their beds. The moose moved silently past them and kept to the far side of several large spruce trees in order to avoid being spotted. The thick bed of spruce needles muffled his steps, and he took special care to avoid stepping on dead branches. The only sound was the cawing of several crows circling above and the whir of some partridge wings as they flew away from him. The next large pond was still a couple of miles away in a depression in the middle of a meadow on the far side of a rocky cliff at the end of the ridge to the east. The moose had fed in that pond last summer, but he had approached it from the north. He'd not passed below the cliff and was not at all aware it was the habitat of a mountain lion.

As the moose traveled northeast toward the cliff, the sun was near the southern horizon as it continued on its journey to the west. Of course at this time of the year, it never moved toward the north the way it did in the summer. Fortunately, the frigid weather meant that the horrible clouds of blackflies, which could drive an animal to the point of madness in the summer, were absent. As the moose moved toward the ridge, he could smell the pond ahead, and his hunger pangs increased. He could just about taste the juicy bulbs. He moved faster, now that he was away from the people in the village, the noise he was making did not matter. However, there was another set of ears that heard even better than humans—those of a mountain lion!

The big "queen" cat heard the moose coming towards her lair even before she was able to see it. She left the cave and her cubs, in order to move to the edge of the cliff where she could leap onto the back of any unsuspecting prey that might pass by. Fortunately for her, the rocky cliff was directly between the moose and the pond, and he was heading right her way. She crouched low at the cliff's edge and hoped the moose would not lift his eyes high enough to spot her. He did not, and the cat made the leap onto the broad back and sunk her claws into each sides of his thick neck. The moose bolted and ran toward the pond. The cat clung on even tighter and bit into the neck just on top of the spine. Her long fangs sank all the way to the spinal cord. The moose dropped onto its front knees and then rolled to one side, paralyzed. The cat then attacked the neck with her claws, severing the artery that delivered blood to the brain. In less than a minute the moose was dead.

Before she could take a bite of choice parts of her fresh kill, the cougar heard the wolves. They had come back to her territory and would be here soon. She instinctively knew she needed to quickly return to the safety of the cliff before they got here! A pack of wolves was not something she cared to fight off for this or any other kill. She knew there would always be another prey to kill.

11 ❖ The Wolves and the Lioness

The young, black wolf woke up from his deep sleep with a familiar feeling. It was a gentle nuzzling on top of his head, and it brought back the memory of his mother doing that when he was just a young pup. Had he been accepted back into the pack that he had just been driven from only two days ago? Was this his mother gently waking him again? He opened one eye and saw it was the young female who, just yesterday, had shared her small meal of tender fawn's leg with him.

He opened his other eye and saw all the members of his new pack standing nearby. The alpha male's bright blue eyes were fixed upon him. The youngster thought, he's staring me down and issuing me a challenge! As a male, that was naturally the black's first thought, but then he saw that the eyes of the rest of the pack were also fixed on him. They were all waiting for him to wake up from his sound sleep, so they could be on their way to another hunt. As far as they were concerned, the meager meal they'd had yesterday was only an appetizer. It was high time for another hunt, and if the young black chose not to join them and wanted to continue sleeping, they would be off without him.

He was instantly awake and sprang to his feet. Being left behind from his first hunt with this new pack was not going to happen. He longed to share another meal of warm flesh with the young female that had gently wakened him. As soon as they saw he was on his feet, the pack was off at a trot, searching for the aroma of a bedded-down doe. Hopefully, they would find one with a fawn as well. The pack was so ravenously hungry that both of the animals would be reduced to scraps of fur, hide and bloodstains in the snow when they were finished with them. One forty-pound wolf could consume close to its own weight at a large kill.

The most successful hunter of the pack was the alpha female that was the mother of the young she-wolf that had just nudged the black wolf to wake him. Besides being often the best hunter, an alpha female was expected to discipline the unruly, young pups that failed to follow the instinctive rules of the pack.

Now, as he observed this alpha female's tracking skills, the black's thoughts went back to the time the alpha female of his pack had put a quick stop to his unruly behavior. She rushed at him at full speed, knocked him off his feet, and nipped him on his exposed tender underbelly.

The young black had been running around nipping the flanks of smaller wolves in a show of his size and aggressive nature that he, as son of the alpha male, felt he needed to prove to the pack. The alpha female had driven him away from the pack for doing this. His isolation and hunger lasted for three days before he had been allowed to crawl back on his belly and finally was allowed to rejoin the circle of wolves as they feasted on a fresh kill of caribou. The experience had been terrifying, because he didn't know if he had been doomed to spend the rest of his life as a lone wolf on account of this bad behavior.

Today, after the female let out a series of yelps to indicate she had scented prey, the pack was off at high speed in a rush to catch up to whatever she might have found. The pack would aid in the kill or would assist in driving off another predator from the kill. She was soon leading them along a trail of fresh footprints. Their shape and size was unlike any the wolf had ever seen or smelled. The paws that left these prints were round, rather than the long shape of a bear print. He saw little signs of claws in the footprint, but he did see traces of dried blood at the front of the print where the claws would be found. This meant the pack was on the trail of a meat eater, not a prey animal. This was a puzzle to him, even though the rest of the pack seemed to know what they were running after.

Now the alpha male moved up to lead the pack once they approached some towering craggy cliffs. A mixture of howls and snarls echoed back along the trail, and when the young black reached the base of the cliffs, he saw the pack had surrounded a tawny-colored animal who had leapt from the ground to a crag twenty feet up the cliff. Even though the black wolf had seen a lynx before, this cat was many times the size of that animal. The cat snarled and spit at the exasperated pack at the base of the cliff. It was soon obvious that this chase had evolved into a stalemate, since the wolves could not climb up to reach the cat, and the cat was not about to come down to fight off the hungry wolves.

Then the pack smelled the blood of the cougar's fresh kill and headed for it. They did not have far to go. It was fortunate there was not a wolverine already feasting there. The tracks surrounding the kill were those of the lioness they had chased to the cliff. Their day was turning out to be perfect—they now had a freshly killed moose carcass all to themselves. The pack quickly started to tear into it, but the alpha male snarled a warning. All of the other members of the pack stepped back, and the alpha female moved in for her choice. The moose had expired with his tongue hanging out. The alpha clamped her powerful jaws down on the tongue, and with one strong twist of her head, tore most of it out. She turned and went over to drop her choice in front of her daughter.

The rest of the wolves, including the alpha male, returned to the carcass and resumed their feasting. The black wolf thrust himself between the sides of two larger wolves, but they paid him no mind. The other wolves had already torn open the body cavity and were tearing loose the organs. This enabled him to tear loose a large piece of liver. It was so juicy and delicious that the black couldn't resist going back for another huge piece. However, instead of eating it himself, he decided to take it over to the young female who had offered to share the small deer haunch with him just yesterday. He saw the gratefulness in her eyes as he laid the juicy morsel in front of her. Then he went back to the moose carcass to tear a few more bites of leg muscle off the carcass before it was down to skin and bones.

Chasing the lion back to the cliff was a natural thing for the wolves to do, because there was always the urge within any canine to pursue any cat. Also, finding and eating the lion's entire kill was a huge bonus for the pack. It was mid-March, and the long winter was not yet over.

Until spring came, there would be little in the way of easy pickings for the wolves. They could go for four or five days without eating, if that were necessary—and it often was! And then there were times when the entire pack might only kill a single snowshoe hare, and each wolf would have to settle for a single mouthful of meat that it was able to violently wrench from the small carcass as it was being torn apart. Such was the law of the north woods in the ongoing struggle for survival during a sub-arctic winter in the Yukon Territory.

12 ❖ The Lioness

The lioness knew that the wolves had left her territory, because they were so noisy as they moved on. They also howled from the top of the ridge across from the valley that she liked to think of as her own private hunting ground. She felt ashamed that she'd allowed the pack to run her up the cliff, but for some reason, wolves or dogs in packs terrified her. She often wondered why she had that fear, because she knew her claws could disembowel one of those dreadful creatures, and her long teeth could bite through their snouts and break both their upper and lower jaws. In spite of that knowledge, there was that old instinct that compelled cats to climb every time they were pursued by canines, because their pursuers could not. Also, canines hunted in packs, and this meant they could attack from all sides at once. As few as two large hounds could tree a lion.

The lioness had little knowledge of dogs and had never been pursued by a pack of them. Dogs seemed less aggressive and far less savage than wolves. However, she recently learned that some breeds of dogs could be more aggressive than others, even if they didn't look it. The lion recalled a recent time when two redbone coonhounds had cornered a male grizzly at the base of this cliff while she watched from above. The bear had just sent the two hounds tumbling with swats of his great paws when a smaller, rust-colored dog with curly hair (an Airedale Terrier) jumped up and locked its jaws on the bear's throat. The bear, which had previously sustained a great wound to its nose, had a hard time breathing with the dog's jaws locked around its windpipe. But he was able to tear the dog loose and fled, with the two hounds chasing him.

The cougar was hungry and was tired of waiting any longer, so she made a leap from her perch and landed about fifteen feet from its base. That was a skill she had practiced when her mother had taught her hunting skills. A leap like that from a tree or cliff could place the lion squarely on the back of a prey animal. After anchoring herself to the animals back by sinking her claws deeply into the prey's skin, she could bite through the thick muscles surrounding the spine and sever the spinal cord. That was how she had killed the moose only hours ago. Now she hurried back to the carcass to see if the wolves had left anything for her to eat.

She found there was nothing left but some shredded skin and blood spots in the snow. Those miserable curs, she thought. They didn't even leave any bones! She lapped up some spots of bloody snow as she glared in the direction they had taken. Why couldn't they make their own kills, instead of taking mine? They were flea-bitten robbers—nothing more than large coyotes that in her mind were just filthy scavengers. Also, now mountain lions had to contend with those crossbreeds, the coywolves! After man had decimated many of the North American continent's wolves with traps and poison baits, some lone male wolves had begun breeding with female coyotes. Their offspring had the size and strength of a wolf and the cunning skills taught by coyote mothers.

Well, she thought, there was nothing left to do except make another kill. She needed food to enrich her body and permit her to return to her den and nurse her two young cubs. She turned in the opposite direction from where the wolves were heading. Their continued howling, intended to drive their prey from their beds, had alerted all the animals in the valley below that hunters were about. This was just the opposite technique used by a hunting lioness. At night she moved silently and slowly through the forest and meadows, counting on her stealthy movements to allow her to come upon any potential prey in their bed. During the daylight hours, she relied on positioning herself in a tree or a rock outcrop above a game trail. If an animal walked by, she could instantly spring onto its back for the kill.

A third way of hunting was to stalk her kill. She had just spied the three white dots of a family of Rocky Mountain goats grazing about five-hundred yards on the hill above her, so that's what she decided to do. She planned to travel up through a ravine filled with aspens in order to flank the goats and get above them. Then she would creep very slowly on her belly, until she could take several bounds downhill and spring onto the back of one of them.

Attacking three mountain goats was not without serious risks, because all of them have sharp, pointed horns. Although they were not long, those horns could still be thrust into the throat or belly of an attacker. The lion decided she would have to make her attack from the rear, hoping that the other two goats would panic and run away from the unlucky victim.

The lion was aware that any other prey might not be found for another day or two. This might be the only meal available to her today, so she would risk it. It was slow going through the aspen ravine that had been littered with dead branches knocked down by many winters of heavy snowfalls. The lioness crept through the tangle of branches in order to minimize the noise that could alarm the goats grazing on the new spring grass about thirty yards to the east of her position. She continued climbing until she was well above them. The ravine ended, and the ground was littered with large boulders. This was very good because they provided extra cover as the lion worked her way back down the hill to close the distance between her and the goats.

It took quite a while to worm her way along the ground, moving from one boulder to another. The sun had moved from its position at high noon to where it usually sat around two o'clock. Unfortunately, as the goats grazed, they moved downhill faster than the lion could stealthily crawl among the boulders. Her prey was now farther away than they were when she had left the cover of the ravine. As she slowly moved her head around another boulder, the lion was shocked to see a golden marmot a foot away. The large rodent had its back to the lion and was intently watching the goats as they devoured what the marmot had planned to eat over the next few weeks.

Now the lion had to decide whether she would either remain still until the marmot decided to go back into its hole beneath the rock, or move forward and risk the probability that the marmot would whistle and alarm the goats. Or she could just eat the marmot and forget the goats. The latter was probably the safest choice. A marmot was larger than a squirrel but smaller than a groundhog. It would satisfy her hunger for the day, so she thrust her head forward and devoured it in two bites. As it expired, its squeals alarmed the goats, and they all disappeared over the breast of the hill. Such was the luck of the hunt!

13 ❖ The Mustang

To look at him, most would bet a good sum that he was a purebred Arabian stallion. You could tell that by the shape of his head, the pale ghostlike body coloring, the black dusting around his narrow nose and large nostrils, and the flowing black mane and tail. He really was a mustang, a mixed breed, although his appearance would lead one to believe otherwise.

Mustangs roam free on unfenced (usually public) lands and aren't domesticated, but unlike most other wild mammals, when given the right opportunity, they can bond with humans. They respond quite readily to gentleness, as opposed to heavy-handed methods of "breaking them in." So, their scientific description of *Equus ferus*—feral horse—is the more accurate term.

Mustangs usually have a mixture of genes (or DNA) from many horses, and the variety of sizes, bone structures and colors are endless. It was unusual to see the typical coloring and traits of a purebred Arabian in a mustang. Was this a domesticated animal that was set free to wander? Even if this was the case, his DNA might be traced back to the time when horses were brought to North America by the first legions of Spanish Conquistadors, or years later when officers accompanying General Santa Ana at The Alamo were felled by well-aimed ball shots from Kentucky rifles and their horses ran off into the surrounding countryside.

So, what was this striking mustang doing here, alone in the Yukon Territory? Was he driven from his herd by a stronger stallion eager to lessen chances of inbreeding or to eliminate competition for brood mares? Did he travel many miles north, following the sun as it moved each spring from northern Alberta to the territory where he found lots of new growth of tender spring grasses?

Or was he following some primal urge to travel toward the land bridge across the Bering Strait, just as the ancient herds of horses did when they migrated across this territory and were bound for new homes in the steppes of what is now Russia? Paleontologists have identified jawbones of small horses found in the Yukon Territory that were thousands of years old, but no herds of feral horses are found there today.

In any case, if he found no horse herds to join up with, he might have been searching for a man, because by nature horses were herd animals that always had the urged to "join up" for protection. And, of course, the Yukon was home to numerous species of predatory animals, so this urge would be an extremely strong one.

It was now early October, and all the lush green grasses of spring and summer had turned dry and tan. All of the native Athabascan women were gathering seeds to mix with animal fat and make seed cakes (pemmican) for the coming winter. The racks of drying salmon were full, and the men were hunting in bands, hoping to find some buffalo that had not already migrated to the south.

The stallion turned his back to the bitter wind from the far north and regretted not being allowed to join the herd of those massive, brown wooly bison as they departed these lands and headed back to Alberta. He faced a huge problem, with little hope of a solution, because there were numerous packs of wolves that he could hear howling on these cold nights. A lone horse was an easy target for any wolf pack to chase down, surround, and kill. Since he was a young male and had not tried to mate with one of the many mares in his former herd, he had no idea why he was not allowed to remain in the herd.

The temperature had dropped at least fifteen degrees after the sun sank below the ridge that evening. The stallion shivered when he heard the first howl of the pack that had just entered the small valley where he'd decided to spend the night. If they smelled his fresh droppings, as he was sure they would, they would be on him in minutes. The only thing to do was to try and leave this area as quietly as possible. The loud clop of his hooves on the rocky ground made this practically impossible.

He had only covered about seventy-five yards when he heard the snarl of the alpha-female wolf just behind him. As she leaped for his hindquarters, the stallion jammed his front legs into the ground and kicked both rear legs back as hard as he could. Both rock-hard hooves struck the wolf, and she fell to the ground in a heap. Her hunting days had come to an abrupt end because she would not survive the fractured skull those hooves had just delivered. The rest of her pack was close behind. The stallion knew he would not be able to deal with their numbers, especially if they were able to surround him.

He saw the light color of a granite cliff just ahead, visible by the light of the full moon. As he reached it, he turned to face the wolf pack. At least his vulnerable hindquarters were protected, and he could deal deadly blows to any wolf that got within range of his hooves. The rest of the pack made a half-circle around the horse as they started to slowly creep towards their intended victim. It was only a matter of seconds before they would all spring forward.

There was a man with a rifle up there, and he began shooting as many wolves as he could before they all fled. He was able to kill four, and then he started to climb down. It was the trapper.

When he reached the bottom, he had a skinning knife in his hand to collect their valuable hides. He found that the terrified horse was still standing at the base of the cliff, wide eyed and trembling. "Easy boy," the trapper said in a soft voice. "You don't need to be afraid of me. I won't hurt you." The horse heard the gentleness in the man's voice and began to calm down.

This man had saved him from the wolves. Maybe this was someone he could join up with for protection. The man busied himself with skinning the wolves while the horse watched. He made quick work of it and then rolled each hide and tied them with cord, so he could carry them back to his cabin, flesh them out, and stake them out for drying tomorrow. As he started walking away, the horse fell in behind him. The trapper turned and said, "Are you going to follow me home? Cause if you do, I am going to have to add a winter stall to the side of my cabin and start putting up lots of dry grass for the winter to feed you. You're a beaut, for sure. You'll turn out to be either a good mount or at least an excellent packhorse soon!"

❖ Epilogue

I hope you enjoyed these wild animal tales, but were they fanciful or true-to-life? It has generally been accepted (by man) that humans are the only species capable of reasoning and rational thought, and that all animals are without intellect and act merely instinctively or in accordance with things they have been taught, either by their parents or, in the case of domesticated animals, by man.

When Jane Goodall lived with and studied a group of chimpanzees in the 1960s, she learned they had tool-making skills, formed family alliances, and were emotionally complicated. Many years later, however, when ethnologist Frans de Waal wrote *Are We Smart Enough to Know How Smart Animals Are?*, many claimed his writings were merely "anthropomorphic, romantic, and unscientific."

Today, science has made many discoveries of animal cognition. A search on Google for "animal" and "cognition" references more than 190,000 "hits" on animal intelligence. Researchers are finding many examples of behaviors by different animal species that indicate they have far greater intelligence than we previously credited them with having.

One animal that has been studied extensively is the black bear. By closely observing a family group of twenty-two bears living near his home in Lyme, New Hampshire,

Ben Kilham, a former biology student and long-time wildlife rehabilitator, discovered that bears are quite social, use a system of communication, are governed by rules of conduct, and form long-term relationships.

To make my point, as a discerning reader, you have no doubt recognized that I believe that there is intelligence that exists in the brains of each of the animals I have written about here. They used reason and logic to fight and survive in a hostile environment that's filled with fierce predators.

Why am I so sure about this degree of animal intelligence? Well, just consider our mixed-breed dog named George (named by our daughters who said they were going to treat him like a brother). George would get excited when he heard me tell my wife that I was going to take him out for our after-dinner walk, and he would start leaping in the air. In order to avoid this scene, I started to spell the word W-A-L-K. George quickly figured what that spelled, and his high jumps immediately resumed! Now George could not spell, but he quickly associated the four letters I was spelling out loud with the evening walks he loved to take with me!

Did the lioness use our language when she thought the wolves were "miserable curs" for devouring her moose kill? No, she probably had something along the lines of those same thoughts in her own "lionese" language. However, because we wouldn't understand that, I had to use English—possibly one of the world's most confusing methods of communication.

So, yes, animals are gifted with sophisticated instincts that have evolved to match their needs and environments, and they have extremely sharp senses. I also think they come closer to having minds, hearts and souls than many of us have ever imagined. Enjoy your forays into the wild—and enjoy your relationships with the animals, both wild and domestic, with which we are blessed to share this planet!

❖ About the Author

Lloyd Shanks has always been an avid reader and gains a lot of satisfaction in writing. During his working career, he sold a number of technical articles to the periodical *Hazmat Packager and Shipper*. After retiring, he contributed several historical articles to monthly publications of the Historical Reno Preservation Society and Sparks Heritage Museum.

This is his first, fully published book. However, in 2005, he did have a first draft of the story *Walking with Mustangs* printed to give to his family and friends. That year, he shared it with another writer on a cruise to Alaska who said it was "heartfelt" and encouraged him to keep working on it and to get it published. Lloyd lives with his family in Bozeman, Montana.

Autographed copies may be purchased
for $14.95 + $3 postage.

Contact the author by email at:
muledeerpress@gmail.com
or by postal mail to:

MULE DEER PRESS
3426 Lemhi Trail Drive
Bozeman, Montana 59718

Also available on Amazon.com